THE LEADER IN YOU

OVIDILIO D. VASQUEZ

SUGARCANE
Publishing

Copyright © 2017
Speak Performance International, LLC
Sugarcane Publishing

ISBN-10: 154420647X
ISBN-13: 978-1544206479

INTRODUCTION

During my six-month internship in Salesforce, a multi-billion company, I remember being given the opportunity to deliver a five to seven-minute presentation to account executives that had traveled from all over the world.

I began my presentation by saying, "Some people don't care who you are unless they know what you do. And some people don't care about what you do unless they know why you do it." In addition, I had once heard and then recounted a striking phrase that said, "When you find your why, you find your way." Simon Sinek, famous speaker, author and professor once proposed a golden circle that begins with "why," "what," and "how." So, let me tell you the reason why I wrote this book.

I am a farm boy from the sugarcane fields of Guatemala. Many people would think that if you are born in a third-world country, you will most likely not be able to make it in the big world. I was born in 1990 and grew up on a farm owned by my grandmother, Elena Sarceño. My grandma, Elena Sarceño, never went to school and did not know how to read or write. Therefore, I want to leave a legacy that makes an impact, hopefully one greater than the impact my grandma made during her life. My grandma helped many people through her hard work, wisdom, and with finances. My grandma helped women during labor when they were pregnant, and she helped them until they were ready to return to their homes with their husbands and the rest of their family.

The main reason I am writing this book is to leave this legacy of positivism, high-quality content, hope, community, and leadership, because when you know your why, you will find your way. As you continue to read this book, you will find strategies, qualities, and reasons why you should develop the leader you were born to be.

I'm going to tell you a little bit about myself. Then I'm

going to go ahead and share with you what to do to possibly find those qualities of leadership, which I am sure you already possess, and only probably just need to be reminded of. I'm also quite sure that you probably already have characters that exhibit these qualities. Then, I'm going to show you how to use these competencies in your journey as a student and young adult, in becoming the professional that you are meant to be, through leadership, focusing on education and what's important to you for your own goals, in order to succeed in this world.

I am reminded of a quote by Earl Nightingale, a very famous motivational speaker and radio broadcaster. He said, "Success is the progressive realization of a worthy ideal." If you are a teacher, a student, a parent, or a professional in various fields, and you enjoy what you do and have fulfillment in doing what you do every day, then you, my friend, are successful.

I am not a Guru. I am a lifelong learner. What I share here with you is just for you to try. If it works for you, great! I do believe this information can dramatically improve the quality of your life. See you at the top! Do what you can, where you are, with what you have.

CONTENTS

ACKNOWLEDGMENTS

These wonderful people have helped me grow into the leader that I am. You see, nobody makes it alone in this world. We all need somebody to stand by us, that person that gives you the, "You've got this" look. It takes a village, my friend. All these leaders have contributed to my growth. They have invested their precious time in me and shared invaluable advice with me. What are the names of the leaders you learn from? List their names in here, make sure to show them appreciation for their dedication to your personal success. A "Thank-you" note will do.

Doña Elena Sarceño Ruiz (My grandmother)
Verónica Avilés Sarceño (My mother)
Pegine Echeverria
Ricardo González
Victor Antonio

A FARM BOY

Once, I walked into a store, checked out a book, and I remember after checking it out, I wasn't really interested in reading it anymore. The main reason was because I did not know anything about the author. The title caught my eye, but the author was unknown to me. I'll give you a little personal back-story so you know who you are learning from. If you want to get right into the content, please, be my guest and skip to the next chapters.

As I said in the introduction, I am a farm boy from the sugarcane fields of Central America. I was born in 1990. My father was killed six months after I was born. I never knew him. His name was Manuel Sagastume. My mother raised my older sister, my younger brother and our youngest brother, who, for reasons unknown to me, died at the age of two years old. Growing up on a farm, in a village where the nearest town was about 45 minutes away traveling by car, I grew up with very limited resources. We only had money to buy one pair of shoes for the entire year. We made sure that those shoes were steel-toe shoes. Steel toe shoes will last us for at least the whole year. Usually, we would buy these shoes during the month of September because Independence Day was in September.

Everyone would dress nicely and we would have a big party on September 15, the Independence Day of my home country, Guatemala.

Growing up in a farm, I had to learn how to milk cows at the age of eight. My Uncle Hector used to teach me how to milk cows. Let me give you a little bit of advice: never spank a cow. Once, when I was probably 10 years old, out of nowhere it occurred to me to spank a cow that was eating grass. As I spanked her, she kicked me right in my stomach and I flew about three to five feet away from where I was standing and slammed my body on the ground, moaning and groaning because of this pain that was killing me. I could not breathe. I could not ask for help. I was the only one there in the field. About five to eight minutes later, I stood up from the ground and swore never to spank a cow again. This, to me, was funny. Now that I'm an adult and thinking back in time, it was just an experience that reminds me that when you do things you're not supposed to, hurtful things can happen to you.

You will observe a picture of me riding a cow in this book. This cow's name was Angela. My mom bought it for me, and I used to take care of it. You'll see the surroundings in the picture: poor land, banana trees all over, no asphalt, pure terrain.

When I was about 14 years old, my mom set up a little grocery store – a convenience store more or less – for me to manage. You'll see a picture of me pointing to the sign that says, "Tienda Panamericana" which means "An American Store". I was very happy, but I never learned about money management, so after a few months, the business went bankrupt.

My mom worked really hard, living in the United States, to send me money to set up this store. My mom used to live in the Bay Area of San Francisco, California. She used to clean houses and banks. She also used to work in warehouses, packaging products.

She was injured at a point and couldn't work for a little while. That's when I had to man up and get to work for real. I had been working my whole life since I was eight when my Uncle Hector used to teach me how to milk cows. I would get up at 5:00 in the morning, walk towards the fields, get the cows rounded up, get the cow I needed, sit right next to the cow and begin milking it. I would also clean around the house with a machete from the ages of 8,

9, 10, 11, 12. Once I had begun, it never stopped.

My culture is probably somewhat like yours. We celebrate different occasions like baby showers, weddings, birthdays, even sweet 16 birthdays – except we do it at 15. We call them Quinceañeras. We make sure we get cake and candles. Everyone gathers up to sing you Happy Birthday in Spanish. You will observe a picture of my brother turning, I believe, 11 or 12 years old, surrounded by my aunt, my cousin, my other cousin and a family friend singing Happy Birthday. You'll also observe a picture where my brother, wearing a blue shirt, is standing next to my cousin with a white t-shirt, holding a phone and making a call. They were calling my mom. She used to live in the United States of America, the land of opportunity, the land where people die on the border, in the desert, just to try to cross into the United States of America.

I know I skipped a few years of my life, from the very beginning until I was around 12 to 14 years old. But growing up from 1 to 12 years old, I had to live in scarcity. I lived a very modest life. I had to live in a place where we did not have electricity until the year 2000 when I was about to turn 10 years old. We used to ride our bicycle about 20 minutes so we could go to the nearest store, buy candles, bring it back home, and then light them up during the night. That was our light source for years, until the year 2000. Times were tough, but then again, as the phrase goes, "When the going gets tough, the tough has to get going." Another phrase that I remember says that "Tough times reveal to a man his true character."

This I did not know when I was young. Then when I grew up, as a young adult, I learned these lessons that I unconsciously knew, practiced, acted out, but was never fully aware of. I want you to be aware of these lessons. I want you to be aware of what's possible for you. I want you to be conscious of the opportunities surrounding you. I encourage you to take a leap of faith when you feel a little bit afraid. Take the dive, make your educational dreams come true, and influence your parents, brothers, sisters, and best friends to help you, encourage you, challenge you, to get the best out of you.

I grew up in a Catholic family. You will observe a picture of me standing next to my grandma in a Catholic church. This church was in a town about an hour and a half from where I was born, and this picture was taken probably in 2013. My grandma meant everything to me.

Later in the book, I'm going to tell you about the story of how I was coming to cross the border in Mexico and I was in jail and my grandma took a trip to come look for me. More details will come later in this book. My grandma,"Mama Lena" was a woman who was respected in our village. Our village had around 300 to 500 people, maximum. All of us worked in the fields. We harvested sugarcane, bananas, mangoes, and planted all those things as well. From planting to harvest, the cycle was repeated over and over again. You will observe a picture of my brother Francisco wearing a "Bad Dog" t-shirt, where he is about 12 years old in the fields. He isn't working, he is just posing for the picture. But where does a 12-year-old belong? In the fields or in an educational institution? Our leadership will grow to the extent that we, ourselves, grow.

When I was 14 years old, I was working in the sugarcane fields of Guatemala. You will observe a picture of me sitting on the motorcycle next to my cousin, Antonio. Antonio used to influence me. He used to be the

leader that would influence me because he was older than me, had more life experience than me, and mainly because he was my family member. We worked together in the fields for a few months before I took the trip to come into the United States of America. That motorcycle in the picture was mine. I learned to ride a motorcycle when I was about 13 years old. No helmet, no license, no rules – just me and my motorcycle.

Probably like your family, we celebrated birthdays, as I mentioned earlier, and we broke piñatas like most Hispanics did. Piñatas are made from paper and are full of candy. You will observe a picture of me breaking a piñata

in front of the kitchen where I used to live. This kitchen was made of wood, very poor, and without running water. We barely had electricity in the year 2000. We didn't even have running water where I was born. We would rather draw water from wells. We would dig a well in every house and buy a bucket… We would then put a stone on one side of the bucket, so when the bucket reaches the water, the bucket leans towards one side and gathers water into it and then you pull it up with a rope. You repeat the process until you get all the water you need for your cooking, laundry, shower, and for every need that you have in a household.

My other grandmother's name is Concepcion, also known as "Doña Conchita." You will observe a picture of her inside a Catholic church next to my sister. My sister is holding my little niece. That was her very first baby. My sister's name is Rubila Gabriela. We were very Catholic until my mind became more exposed at 11 years old and I learned about new religions and decided to branch out from it. But this book is not about religion or beliefs.

This book is about leadership, and now I am just telling you a little bit about myself. Continue reading so you can see what makes my "why". You will observe a picture of several kids next to a piñata. These kids were celebrating a birthday for one of my nieces. Her name was Karen. To me, kids are very meaningful in this world.

You will also observe a picture of my three nieces. Now I have four. They are Elvia, Dulce, and Katy. They mean everything to me. I work day and night to make sure they are doing well, healthy, and they are going to school.

That's a little about my family, a little bit about my background. In the next chapter, you will learn a little bit about my journey coming to the United States of America.

"The roots of education are bitter, but the fruit is sweet."

~ Aristotle

Based on my story growing up, what do we have in common? Share your thoughts about this chapter.

_____
_____
_____
_____
_____
_____
_____
_____
_____
_____
_____
_____
_____
_____
_____
_____
_____
_____
_____
_____
_____
_____
_____
_____
_____
_____
_____
_____
_____
_____
_____

Based on my story growing up, what do we have in common? Share your thoughts about this chapter.

_____
_____
_____
_____
_____
_____
_____
_____
_____
_____
_____
_____
_____
_____
_____
_____
_____
_____
_____
_____
_____
_____
_____
_____
_____
_____
_____
_____
_____
_____
_____

Based on my story growing up, what do we have in common? Share your thoughts about this chapter.

_____

_____

_____

_____

_____

_____

_____

_____

_____

_____

_____

_____

_____

_____

_____

_____

_____

_____

_____

_____

_____

_____

_____

_____

_____

_____

_____

_____

_____

_____

_____

_____

_____

_____

_____

Based on my story growing up, what do we have in common? Share your thoughts about this chapter.

_____

_____

_____

_____

_____

_____

_____

_____

_____

_____

_____

_____

_____

_____

_____

_____

_____

_____

_____

_____

_____

_____

_____

_____

_____

_____

_____

_____

_____

_____

_____

_____

_____

Based on my story growing up, what do we have in common? Share your thoughts about this chapter.

_____
_____
_____
_____
_____
_____
_____
_____
_____
_____
_____
_____
_____
_____
_____
_____
_____
_____
_____
_____
_____
_____
_____
_____
_____
_____
_____
_____
_____
_____

COURAGE

You may be familiar with my journey to the United States of America because you probably experienced it yourself or have a friend or family member or know someone who has gone through a journey similar to the personal one I will share with you.

When I was 15, my mom called me and asked if I wanted to come to the United States. I said, "Yes, of course." Like most young people in a third-world country, we dreamed of coming to the United States, the land of opportunities. I made the journey by taking buses with a friend of mine to come through Mexico, but on the first bus that I caught in Mexico, after I crossed the Guatemalan border, immigration in Mexico found out that I was not Mexican, and because I was a young adult, they put me in a jail for young adults.

In this place where a lot of other young adults were, we had to eat cold food, unsalted rice and sometimes, they would bring warm food that had somewhat of seasoning in it with tortillas. With me, there were about 60 other young adults from all over the world – Nicaragua, Honduras, Panama, Brazil and other countries – that were chasing the American dream just like I was.

At this point, I called my mother. She was in the United States. I explained to her what had happened. I had gotten caught while sitting in a bus traveling through Mexico and I needed money because I wanted to buy some of the snacks that they sell in those places where they keep you so you do not leave or try to move onwards through Mexico. My mom had no way to send me money because I was only 15. I didn't have the right documents to be able to receive money that was transferred from a different country and I was getting desperate.

By this time, we already had electricity in my village, and my uncles had put a phone in my grandma's house. So my mom called my grandma and explained everything that had been happening at that time. My grandma, being the brave, caring, loving and absolutely amazing grandma that she was, made the trip from Guatemala; from a village far away from any town, far away from the state, without knowing how to read or write. She made the trip to Mexico to try and find me.

She arrived at the border of Guatemala and Mexico and she couldn't get any farther. She had to travel back all the way across the whole country to her old house, where she was devastated, sad, in tears, and hurt because she had failed in her mission to find me and take me back home to a safe place.

Let me ask you a question: who in your family cares most about you? Acknowledge this person. In your leadership journey, make sure that your impact resembles and reflects all these positive traits. All these positive impacts this person has on you are reflected in the positive impact you make on others on your path to success as a student, professional, and an asset to your community rather than a liability. I am reminded of the phrase that says, "If you want to be seen as an asset to your community rather than a liability, dress like a prospect rather than a suspect."

My grandma failed to find me in Mexico but she waited patiently as the wise and patient woman that she was. They do say that patience is a virtue and she was virtuous. After some time being held at that place, a guy from Nicaragua assaulted me. He grabbed a pointy piece of metal, put it against my neck and threatened to kill me if I did not give him all the money I had and a wristwatch I was wearing. I informed him that I had no money, and that I had worked hard to buy the watch I then had on my left hand, and I was not going to give it to him.

He then proceeded to call two of his friends from the same country, and they made sure I gave him the watch. I did, and as I walked out of that dark little room, I talked to some other people from Guatemala, some other young adults, and I told them what had happened. They went on to tell me that they also had been robbed by the same person, but everyone was afraid to tell on him, to tell the guards and the immigration staff that he had been robbing people.

We all summoned courage and spoke to the person in the immigration office. We explained to them. We said, "We are being harassed. We are being robbed. Our lives have been threatened. They stole all the goods that we had, all our belongings, and we don't want to be here anymore. We don't want to be here with this person anymore." We found out that he was over 18 years old and he stayed where only under 18-year-olds were allowed. After immigration took action, they put him in a separate room without a roof, bed, bed sheet, and he was in the cold. Unluckily for him, it rained really hard that day and poured on him. We felt sorry for him, but if immigration agents were not taking him out of that room, then there was nothing we could do for him.

A few days later, they sent me out on a bus from Mexico to Guatemala. My aunt's husband, Sergio, went to pick me up at a place in Guatemala for refugees where they treated me well. They fed me well. They dressed me well, and it was comfortable. I went back to my own village, sad, with my head down, thinking that I failed in my mission to travel to the United States. At only 15 years of age, having the courage, displaying grit, being optimistic, taking risks, putting my life on the line, and I had failed. It was a sad time in my life.

A few months later, my mom called me again and she says, "Do you want to try again?" As you can imagine, a guy, young, ready, and hungry, optimistic, looking forward to the future, wanting opportunities, smart... Even though I only went to sixth grade in my home country, I knew I was smart. I had it in me. I said, "Yes."

My mom said, "In a few days, I'm going to send for you and someone will come pick you up." A guy from Mexico came to pick me up and traveled with me through the whole country of Guatemala and of Mexico. We lived in his house in Puebla Mexico for about a month so I could learn how to speak like the Mexicans, because even though we both speak Spanish, a lot of words are different. The differences in pronunciations and accent could as well tip people off that you're not from around there.

The guy and I traveled privately in buses, bribing immigration officers, until I arrived at Tijuana, Mexico, at the border of San Diego. He left me there in a house with some lady, her husband and her kids. I was there for a few days. They fed me three times a day, two plates each time. I couldn't believe how much these kids ate, but I knew in my mind that it was part of my journey.

I am telling you. You may be going through very strange times. You may be going through turbulent times. You may be going to uncertain times. You may be doubting yourself. You may have to deal with people who you've never dealt with before. You may have to get back up from a previous failure. You may have to go through a path that is unknown to you, but at that moment, you have to stick to your goal and move forward.

A few days later, they talked to another guy who was going to be my guide through the Mexican border so I could cross into the United States. We began our journey with a guy and five more people. They fed us and they said, "Take one gallon of water, that's all you're going to need. You're going to walk six hours and you're going to be in the United States of America." I could feel it – I was anxious, I was happy, I was optimistic, I was eager. I was a 15-year-old full of adrenaline, ready to take on that walk in hot soil, in the cold night. I was ready to make the sacrifice.

I am asking you: through your educational journey, through your professional journey, be ready. Step your two feet on the ground, flat, feel the earth underneath you, feel the energy around and within you and use it. Get optimistic. Get energetic. Become fearless. We walked for six hours through the desert. Sometimes we would stop to drink water or take a 10 to 15-minute rest in a hot sunny day. It was sweltering hot, as hot as a potato – hotter than that actually. After six hours, we talked to our guide and we told him, "You said we were walking for only six hours. Are we there yet?" He responded, "No, we have to walk a few more hours."

We decided to continue moving forward. Getting into the night, we began running out of water. We certainly had no food. Our energy was declining. Our optimism was decreasing. Our hopes were disappearing. During the night we kept walking. A lady that was coming with us began fainting. Her boyfriend asked the guide for help and requested that we would rest every time his girlfriend was fainting. Our guide told him that nobody in our group was a doctor and that we were all in the same situation. Imagine what a tough time that was.

After about 10 hours of walking, it was well into the night. We asked if we could sleep. The guy said we could sleep for two hours maximum because we needed to continue walking, and then, he told us a truth we did not expect. He proceeded to say, "I have a confession to make. I don't know where we are. I've never been in this place before. This is my first time crossing a group of people like you guys." "Oh, no," we said. We were devastated. We lost all hope. We were sad, angry and fearful. The opposite of how we began when we began walking nearly 12 hours earlier.

One of the guys coming with us mentioned that he had been there before, that he had crossed the border many times before, that he knew where to go to, and that if we trusted him, he would guide us. Even our main guide said, "Yes, let's go." We continued walking for miles and miles, mountain after mountain, cliff after cliff. It was a dangerous trip. I wouldn't take this trip again even if someone paid me.

I want to tell you this, maybe the times now are tough for you. Maybe you feel like you're falling off a cliff. Maybe you feel like there are no more resources available for you. Maybe you feel like the person who's been guiding you doesn't even know where to guide you to anymore, just like it happened to me. Maybe you're feeling all alone. Maybe you need answers. Maybe you feel like there is no hope, but I want you to know that at the end of the tunnel, there is light. This, I know you already know. You're probably already familiar with it, but it is true. Even when times seem darkest, the light can shine the most in the darkest place.

Read my next chapter so you can find out about my life experiences in the United States after I had successfully crossed the border, because a few hours after everything I shared with you in the previous pages, we found a freeway where we could be picked up. They picked us up in a truck. They gave us water. They took us to a house in Los Angeles, California. While we were there, they called up my mom living in the San Francisco Bay Area, six hours and a half away from Los Angeles, California. She made the trip from San Francisco, California to Los Angeles, California to go pick me up.

In my next chapter, I'll describe all the details about my experience living in the United States.

"A leader is a dealer in hope."

~ Napoleon Bonaparte

How do you use your courage to help you move forward?
Write down your thoughts on this chapter.

_____

_____

_____

_____

_____

_____

_____

_____

_____

_____

_____

_____

_____

_____

_____

_____

_____

_____

_____

_____

_____

_____

_____

_____

_____

_____

_____

_____

_____

_____

How do you use your courage to help you move forward?
Write down your thoughts on this chapter.

_____

_____

_____

_____

_____

_____

_____

_____

_____

_____

_____

_____

_____

_____

_____

_____

_____

_____

_____

_____

_____

_____

_____

_____

_____

_____

_____

_____

_____

How do you use your courage to help you move forward?
Write down your thoughts on this chapter.

_____
_____
_____
_____
_____
_____
_____
_____
_____
_____
_____
_____
_____
_____
_____
_____
_____
_____
_____
_____
_____
_____
_____
_____
_____
_____
_____
_____
_____
_____
_____

How do you use your courage to help you move forward?
Write down your thoughts on this chapter.

_____

_____

_____

_____

_____

_____

_____

_____

_____

_____

_____

_____

_____

_____

_____

_____

_____

_____

_____

_____

_____

_____

_____

_____

_____

_____

_____

_____

_____

How do you use your courage to help you move forward?
Write down your thoughts on this chapter.

_____

_____

_____

_____

_____

_____

_____

_____

_____

_____

_____

_____

_____

_____

_____

_____

_____

_____

_____

_____

_____

_____

_____

_____

_____

_____

_____

_____

_____

_____

AN OPEN MIND

Leadership is about identifying an opportunity and being able to influence other people to support you when you want to explore this opportunity for yourself so you can make an impact in your community, which includes your family, your friends and everyone else that is around in your schools, in your workplace and the places you visit most – those people that are with you in one way or another.

I arrived in the United States, finally making it, nearly 16 years old. You will see a picture of my mom standing in front of a blue Ford Mustang. My mom's name is Veronica Aviles. She was about 33, maybe 35 years old, at the time of this picture. Then you'll find a picture of myself standing right in front of a wall.

Behind me there is a plant. I was just there, unaware of what the future had in store for me as a new immigrant in the United States of America.

You will also see a picture of me standing next to a young girl, who was nine years old at the time, and whose name I cannot remember any longer. We were coming out of a buffet, a restaurant where you get to choose anything you want from all the several choices of foods they have ready made for you. I was astonished to see so much food, so much variety, all at once, ready to eat. You could eat and after you eat, you would then pay. That was a whole new experience, my very first time eating at a buffet in the United States. In these pictures, I was probably a week into living in the United States. It was only a week after I first arrived.

Around August 2007, I remember my mom took me to a thrift store and I saw a pair of roller-skates. A memory came back to me when I used to watch the movies on television when I was in Guatemala and in these movies, I would see people using roller-skates. I wanted a pair for myself then, but since we did not have any asphalt – the streets were only made of dirt and it was not a smooth surface – I could never buy a pair of roller-skates.

However, this time I had $20 in my pocket while I was browsing through the store, and I knew that it was the right time for me to purchase those roller-skates since I already lived in the United States.

You will observe a picture of me lying on the floor, wearing my first ever pair of roller-skates and yes, I did fall a few times and almost broke my arm during my learning process, but it was fun. It was rewarding. It was part of living my dream.

Ask yourself, "What are some of my dreams?

What are some of the limitations that are currently in my life?

What possible solutions can I come up with to remove these limitations?"

Ask yourself, "Who can I talk to? Who should I seek out advice from?

Who should I partner up with, so I can achieve one, two, or three, or four, or all of the dreams that I have for myself that I currently see limitations for?"

Because these dreams can come true when we find the right people to speak with, when we find the right strategy, when we find the right solution. I've learned the importance of visualization – where you see yourself in the future and begin working towards that future.

As leaders, we must develop self-discipline. The first person that ever taught me to be disciplined was my grandmother. She was very strict. However, her love was two or three times greater than her strictness.

She would tell me that I wouldn't get food unless I got work done. The work that she was referring to was labor work. I had to go around the house, clean it up. Clean up the dry leaves on the yard. Go around, feed the pigs. Go around, feed the cows. Sometimes, we would give the cows food with salt. I never really knew the reason for it, but I knew that we, every now and then, had to give them salt.

Everything else was taken care of besides the water because we had to use a bucket, a big one, to draw out several buckets full of water from a well by hand to be able to store this water, so when the cows were thirsty, they would come and drink this water.

My grandma taught me discipline and hard work – two very important behavioral traits that when you know you work hard in a very disciplined way, you can achieve unbelievable results. I once heard a man saying at a conference that Japanese people are some of the most disciplined people in the world and therefore, they are leaders in many industries.

Ask yourself, "Who am I learning discipline from? Who am I learning hard work from?

Who do I look up to that I believe is a hardworking person?"

Go ahead and write down the names of these people. Go ahead and write down the names of these dreams you came up with earlier. I say names because we have to name our dreams sometimes. Coming to the United States was the American dream. That was the name of my dream.

Sometime in 2008, I experienced bullying at work. I used to work at a warehouse where there were about 50 to 70 employees, and there was this man who would bother me all the time because I was the youngest person working in the warehouse. He would call me names and he would make fun of my accent, and he would laugh because I would try to speak English, when I was barely learning how to speak English.

It came to a point where I said, "Enough is enough." I decided to join a martial arts school in Hayward, California. The name of the school was US Karate. I decided to learn how to defend myself, just so in case I lost my mind and challenged this guy to a fight, because he would bother me every single day at work. I wanted to be prepared.

I'm not encouraging you to prepare yourself to fight a person, but ask yourself, "How am I preparing myself for the challenges that are yet to come?

How did I prepare myself for the challenges that I am facing right now?"

Write down new strategies you can come up with, so you can use them to solve new problems.

I remember a quote from an unknown person that says, "The knowledge that got me here won't get me there." It's very important that you take some time to write down these strategies, so you can reference them, because we tend to forget with time.

You will observe a picture of myself next to my mom, where I'm wearing a martial arts uniform. I stopped going there once I thought I was good enough to defend myself against this guy. Eventually, what happened was I challenged him to a fist fight. He knew that I had been going to martial arts schools for a while then, and he

decided to tell me that he was only joking with me. Throughout all these months, his way of joking with me was not funny to me. Prepare yourself for the challenges that are yet to come, and as a leader, take full responsibility for solving the problems that you will face because we all face problems.

I remember a quote by Albert Einstein that said, "We cannot solve the problems with the same thinking that we used to create them." I am not saying that you are creating your own problems, but all I am saying is to expand your knowledge. Expand your consciousness. Expand your ability to analyze and to act decisively.

You will observe a picture of myself celebrating my 18th birthday. I'm wearing a leather jacket. There's a cake in front of me. My cousin is  standing somewhat next to me. I was very happy. 18 years old, I was an adult now. My mom could not beat me anymore – or so I thought. She was always on my case. I was still working at the warehouse, learning as much as I could to speak English and to make things happen for myself.

You will also observe a picture of my mom, my uncle's wife, my grandma, and my uncle, and three other people in the back of the picture. This picture was taken in 2009. I was struggling my way through high school. My mom was in Guatemala. I was living by myself here in the United States, going to school at 8 am, getting off at 3:30 pm, going to work at 7 pm, getting off work at 2 am, and it was on a daily basis. These were some of the toughest times in my life.

Ask yourself, "What tough times have I survived? What is it that I have been able to conquer?"

These challenges may have seemed big, humongous, enormous, or impossible for you to overcome, and yet you are a victor.

During this time, my grandmother, Elena Sarceño passed away. I remember receiving a call. I was in my History class, US History. When I saw the phone call, I saw the phone number was an international phone number, so I knew the call was from Guatemala. I picked up the call, hiding, so the teacher wouldn't catch me using my cell phone during class.

When my mom spoke to me through the phone, she said, "Mijo," and then I heard a crying voice. "Son," she said again, "Your grandmother just passed away." There was the pause that gives you the chills, and you feel an energy going back and forth in your body, from the top of your head to your toes, and I began to cry. I wanted to walk out of class because I didn't want anyone else to see me cry.

I was an 18-year-old boy, still in high school, still learning English, living by myself. My grandmother, the woman I loved most, even more than my mom, had passed away, and I saw the world coming down on me. I could not do anything to help the situation, so I walked out of class that day and went home and slept through the entire day, but I overcame this challenge.

I am going to ask you, what were your thoughts when you were going through hard times? What was your possible gateway out of that situation, to get out of that mindset? I went straight home and slept because I knew if I was sleeping, I wouldn't be overcome by stress. I'll admit it was very hard for me to go to sleep, but I was so exhausted from working at night every day, that it was actually possible for me to sleep, even though I was very sad.

I made the decision to quit school. I was going to become a dropout. I went to talk to my counselor, Ms. Vasquez, and I told her what had happened and I told her how I felt – devastated, heartbroken, lost, lonely, homesick. I said, "I can't do it anymore. I have got to get out of this school."

She went ahead to persuade me and tell me that I now spoke some English, that I could defend myself, that if there was one way to success, it was through education, and that if I had come up to my grandma and asked my grandma if it was okay for me to quit school because I was going through hard times, what would my grandma have said?

When I gave it some thought, I knew that if I had come up to my grandmother and said, "Mama Lena, I'm quitting high school," she would've looked me straight in the eyes and said, "Are you stupid, boy? We have all sacrificed our lives, so you could get a better education. Don't quit on me. You were not born a quitter. You were born a winner. Because winners never quit and quitters never win. You have my last name. You represent our family. You have my blood. I never thought of you as one to give up. I thought you'd persevere. I thought you to have the courage to develop the strength to keep on keeping on regardless of how tough times would get. I love you, grandson. Don't quit on me."

After I thought of those words that my grandma would have said to me, based on what I knew about my grandmother, I decided to make a commitment. I made a decision. I made up my mind. I was going to do it, not for myself anymore, but I was going to do it for my grandmother, for her pride, for her courage, for her legacy.

I was going to carry on the torch. I was going to light up the fire in my heart to remember what I was made of, that I had her blood in me, that I was going to make her proud because even though she could not see me all the way from Guatemala when she was alive, now she could see me all the way from heaven, where she was now in a better place.

I ask you, what is it that you're going to think about in those tough times, in those moments when you feel like life has knocked you down? You just have to land on your back and look up because if you can look up, you can get up. Write down those reasons why you will never quit. Write down those reasons of why you will always persevere. Write down those compelling reasons why you were born to win.

As time went by, I faced all the struggles. I was once pulled over by the police at 3 in the morning around 2010. The police pulled me over. He said, "May I have your driver's license please?" I said, "No, officer, I don't have one." He said, "Can I see your registration and insurance?" I handed him the registration and insurance. He had pulled me over because I was driving faster than the speed limit. He came back to me and he said, "Son, if you do not have a driver's license, I'm going to have to give you a ticket for speeding, and I'm going to have to take your car."

I had to take out my backpack, my books, and my

lunch from the car. I also took out my 12-inch speakers that I had so I could listen to music. I took them out, put them on the side of the road, and I watched as the police called a towing car and they towed my car away, and then I stayed there on the street at 3 in the morning, all by myself, not knowing what was going to happen next. I called a friend of mine. I explained to him what had happened. He was undocumented like me, so he knew how that felt, and he came on my rescue.

Ask yourself, "Who are the people that I can reach out to, that will understand my pain, that will understand my struggle, that will understand my situation, that will understand my vision, that will understand my goals?

Who are these people that I can reach out to and say these three powerful words, "I need help"?"

These three powerful words can open doors for you. These three powerful words can give other people the chance to help someone else in need. I was in need. I was in pain. I felt lost. I felt like I had nowhere else to go, nothing else to do, but I found hope in someone else's ability to help me.

Finally, I find out that I was not going to be able to graduate on time because I didn't have enough credits to be able to graduate, and then I asked the counselor, "What can I do? What are some strategies that I can adopt? Who do I learn from? Who do I look up to? Who do I ask questions from? Can I get a mentor? Can I get a partner? Can I get a study buddy?" She went ahead to tell me some strategies that could help me graduate on time because I only had three years of high school.

I had never gone to 7th grade, 8th grade, and 9th grade. I was only put in the grade that I was in because I was already 17 years old, and in California, there's a law that you go to the grade according to your age.

The strategy I employed to be able to graduate on

time was this. Classes would usually begin at 8:30 and end at 3:30 pm, so I decided to go to a class before class would begin. I would get to school at 6:30 am. I would stay after school from 4 pm to 5:30 pm, studying hard. I would go to summer school, and take whatever classes there were.

I finally graduated on June 8th, 2011. I made it happen. You will observe a picture of my graduation. You will also see a picture of myself hugging my uncle, Juan Cruz and another picture of myself hugging my aunt, Gabriella Cruz.

I have been through struggles. I have experienced victory. I have been through the growth process. I have been in those places where it's tough to get up from. Let me ask you a question. Are you ready? Are you ready to make your dream happen? Graduating high school was just one of my dreams. Are you ready to make your family proud? Are you ready to say, "Mom, I'm graduating this day"? Are you ready to begin to think about college? Are you ready to prepare yourself for a higher education? Are you ready?

I hope the answer is yes. If the answer is maybe or no, then use the strategies that I used myself, that I have shared with you up until now, to begin to find the answers to your questions, identify the solutions to your problems, come up with ideas and develop competencies that will help you resolve all the challenges that you may now be facing. You are strong. You know you are strong. That's why you have made it this far.

I hope I have inspired you to continue to move forward, and I am not done yet. I encourage you to continue reading this book. I'm going to share with you some of the core competencies of leadership that will help you identify, "Do I have this competency? If I do not have this competency, how can I develop it? Do I have this skill? If I do not have this skill, do I know someone who has this skill that can share with me a strategy, so I can also develop it myself, so I can adapt a new behavior?"

I'm going to share with you everything I think is needed for you to enroll in higher education. I will share with you how it was that I was actually able to make it into college, being undocumented, having a 2.8 GPA from high school, living by myself. See you in the next chapter.

"The challenge of leadership is to be strong, but not rude; be kind, but not weak; be bold, but not bully; be thoughtful, but not lazy; be humble, but not timid; be proud, but not arrogant; have humor, but without folly."

~ Jim Rohn

What strategies do you use, to adapt in a new environment? Share your thoughts about this chapter.

_____
_____
_____
_____
_____
_____
_____
_____
_____
_____
_____
_____
_____
_____
_____
_____
_____
_____
_____
_____
_____
_____
_____
_____
_____
_____
_____
_____
_____
_____
_____
_____

What strategies do you use, to adapt in a new environment? Share your thoughts about this chapter.

_____
_____
_____
_____
_____
_____
_____
_____
_____
_____
_____
_____
_____
_____
_____
_____
_____
_____
_____
_____
_____
_____
_____
_____
_____
_____
_____
_____

What strategies do you use, to adapt in a new environment? Share your thoughts about this chapter.

_____
_____
_____
_____
_____
_____
_____
_____
_____
_____
_____
_____
_____
_____
_____
_____
_____
_____
_____
_____
_____
_____
_____
_____
_____
_____
_____
_____
_____
_____
_____
_____
_____

What strategies do you use, to adapt in a new environment? Share your thoughts about this chapter.

_____
_____
_____
_____
_____
_____
_____
_____
_____
_____
_____
_____
_____
_____
_____
_____
_____
_____
_____
_____
_____
_____
_____
_____
_____
_____
_____
_____
_____
_____
_____
_____

What strategies do you use, to adapt in a new
environment? Share your thoughts about this chapter.

_____

_____

_____

_____

_____

_____

_____

_____

_____

_____

_____

_____

_____

_____

_____

_____

_____

_____

_____

_____

_____

_____

_____

_____

_____

_____

_____

_____

_____

WIN

The most uncertain time in my life was June 2011. I had just graduated high school. Here's what happened next during this time in my life – a lot of uncertainty, confusion and wondering what was next for me. After working in the warehouse that I have worked at for the last five years, one time my car broke down in the street. It was a Chevy Cavalier '95, and I pushed it down to the nearest parking spot I could find, and then left it parked there. I came up with the idea to write a note and put it on my windshield in case they wanted to tow my car. The next day, I went to work walking. I was working on my shift and after a few hours I received a call. The person on the other side of the phone call said that if I did not pick up my car within the next hour, it was going to be towed away. I spoke with my supervisor named Sabir. I told him what had happened, and that I had to leave my car parked in an unauthorized place.

He allowed me permission to leave the job before the shift was finished, and as I was walking out of the warehouse, the manager saw me and asked me where I was going. I explained to him the situation, and that I had asked for permission to leave, and he looked at me, and said, "You can't leave until you finish your job." At that moment, I was very angry. I was frustrated. I was sad, because I was being misunderstood, and because my car was not working, and I was about to walk out of the job, so I did. I turned around and walked out. As I was walking out the door, my manager yelled at me and said, "If you get out of that door, don't come back." That was how I lost my first job here in the United States. Even though they called me back a few days later to see if I still wanted to go and work there, I felt strongly about my dignity that I decided that I did not have to go back to that job.

I began looking for a new job, something new to do. I wasn't going to sit around my house and do nothing. I knew I couldn't go to college because I didn't have enough money, and because I was still undocumented at this point in my life. I had nobody else to count on but myself. I found a job doing sales. In this job, my task was to go to the office in the morning, pick up cans of wax for vehicles, drive to a gas station that I was assigned to, set up a table with a lot of bottles full of wax and spray so I could sell it to potential customers as they came in to fill up their car with gas. Here I learned how to communicate with people, how to persuade people, how to read people, how to be more patient with people, how not to judge people. I learned how to be more persistent. Let me ask you a question. What skills have you learned at a job that you have had before? What are the skills that you can potentially learn at a job that you can have after high school, or right before college, or during high school or college?

Don't think about the job itself. Don't think about how much you're getting paid only. Think about the skills that you are learning. The art of communicating with people, the art of not judging people, the art of reading people, the art of being able to manage your mood regardless of how rude a person is to you so you can speak to the next person as if they are the first person that you're speaking to in that day, in a very friendly manner. Showing charisma, and showing a positive attitude, takes art. Take a moment to write down some of the skills that you have learned in previous jobs that will help you identify what your assets are. Remember these whenever the time comes when you have to write your resume to apply for a job. You can write these skills down that will serve you to build up your value that you will bring to your potential employer.

My second job was working in construction. After working selling wax for cars at gas stations, they sent me to a city called Fresno in California. In this city, it was very hot. The weather was not favorable for me, and I decided to stop working at that job even though I was pretty good at it. I decided to talk to my uncle and ask him if he knew where I could get a job. He works in construction. He has over 20 years of experience, and he told me that I should join the team that he was working on in that company, so I did. I worked in the carpentry section. I used to build walls, hammering down nails, hammering in nails by the hundreds every day. Sometimes it was very, very cold, and the tip of my fingers would feel painful every time I would reach out and grab the wood. Sometimes it was very hot, where I had to continuously drink water so I wouldn't get dehydrated. What I really disliked most about the construction job was the portable restrooms. I certainly did not like that one.

Ask yourself, "What are some of the jobs that I've done that other people would possibly not do? What have I learned from it? What did I do with it, and what can I learn from this experience and my behavior in the past, so that in the next career move that I make, in the next challenge that I take on, I can behave better? How can I make it more to my advantage?" After working with my uncle for about four months, I decided that it was time for me to make a change, because I saw that was going nowhere for me. As I would work throughout the day on the construction site, I would listen to motivational audiobooks. I would listen to motivational speakers like Brian Tracey, Zig Ziglar, Tony Robbins, Victor Antonio, and others that I really liked, like Les Brown. After I decided to quit the job, I decided ... I looked for a different job, and this time, I found a job as a computer technician. I was working for Apple through a third-party agency.

I did not know much about computers besides how to browse the internet, check my email, upload pictures, download music, put music on my phone, edit a few videos for my family members, and that was all I knew. In this company I worked for, they only paid me $12 an hour because I was still undocumented. They took advantage of my skills because they knew I didn't have the right documents to work. I learned how to fix computers and refurbish them to fix any type of problem they had. I would leave them working as if they were brand-new. I received my certification about three times, and even became a trainer to train other computer technicians. I did this computer technician work around 2013. Some of the skills I learned there were to be open-minded, to be teachable, to be coachable. Since I didn't know about this field, I decided to open my mind, be patient, and listen more.

There is a phrase that says, "You have two ears and one mouth. Use them proportionately," so I decided to listen more than I would talk, and I could learn faster. Now, ask yourself, "What are some of the situations that I have been in in which I had to speak out? What are some of the times that I can remember where I had to listen more, so I could absorb the knowledge from others around me that were more knowledgeable than myself?" These are skills that you have developed that you may not be taking account for. The ability to speak up, that is a leadership skill. The ability to listen, that is a leadership skill. The ability to observe and adapt according to what's going on in your environment, and then lead others to change, that is a leadership skill. I want to help you identify the leader in you. My mission is to inspire you. I promised myself that I would leave a legacy just like my grandma did.

After working as a computer technician, I realized that I was being underpaid, and I was tired of it. I decided to make my next move. In 2013, towards the end of the year, I decided to start my own company, Speak Performance International. With only $372, I started my company in the United States. I was beginning to live the American dream. My plan was to speak at different places, telling my story, just like I am doing right now, but instead of through a book, I would do it through speech. A company that I had worked for before during an after-school program found out that I was a public speaker, and that I was available for hire, so they called me and I began working in the Alameda County Office of Education, a local county office of education. I worked there teaching workshops on job readiness skills for at-risk youth. These youths were 18 to 24 years old, and some of them had been in jail. Some of them had been in foster care. Some of them had no parents. Some of them were abused.

These youths had been through hell and back, and my job was to teach them how to be ready for a job. Since I was a young guy, I could easily relate to them. I worked there for a few months until they ran out of budget because this company was nonprofit. I began working at an auto sales job, but before that, I realized that I had learned some skills. I learned how to have compassion for people, how to have empathy. I learned to listen more. I learned to make myself more vulnerable, to share with them some things that I would sometimes not share with other people, and that's how I could truly connect with them. I shared with them my daily struggles. I shared with them my past struggles, and they were able to feel for me just as much as I was able to feel for them. Can you think of a time when you had to make yourself vulnerable so you could get to that level where you can connect to the person next to you?

If you can think of that time, I invite you to write down what was happening that day, and what skills can you identify that you made use of during that time. Again, take count of these skills so you can use them later in your resume, because in the professional world, it's all about dealing with people just as much as it is when you're still in school, when you're at home, when you're at the store, pretty much everywhere. I eventually began working at a dealership, selling cars. This dealership had about 19 cars in the lot, all used vehicles, and my job was to sell people the cars, to get them approved, work with the banks, and do whatever I could to make sure they get the car so I could get my commission. I learned that numbers are very important. I also learned that sometimes you cannot get what you want because the results that you have right now do not measure up to what it is that you think that you desire at this point in your life.

You need to first learn more, so you can become more, and then you can earn more. I learned this lesson from Jim Rohn. After working at this dealership for a while, I realized that selling cars was not for me. Sales were low because marketing was not helping us become known in the town that we were in, in San Leandro, California. In 2014, I applied to get my DACA, Deferred Action for Childhood Arrivals. DACA is a program that allows people that came to the United States at a young age to apply for work authorization. I was lucky enough to get approved for this, and I received my work authorization. I became happy. I felt like I had made it. Many people told me not to apply for this, but I went for it. I had summoned courage. I made a decision based on what I desired and not based on what I feared. Take a moment and think to yourself, "Are all the decisions that I have made based on what I wanted, or based on what I fear?"

F. forget
E. everything
A. and
R. run

F. face
E. everything
A. and
R. rise

More often than not, we find ourselves making the wrong decisions because of the purpose we give it. When we make the right decisions, those are the ones that make the biggest impact in our lives, for the better. As a leader, take a moment to analyze what it is that you want out of your life. You have to make a target so you can hit it. This target will be your goal, and your goal can be one of your dreams. The way it becomes your goal is you set up a date for it, and even though you don't know how it is going to happen, you have to put a date so you can begin thinking of ways to make it happen by that date. That is going to be your target, and therefore you're going to have something to shoot for. Even though I received my DACA, I decided to work part-time at a pizzeria. I used to make pizzas. I used to prepare the ingredients to make these pizzas. I used to be a cashier. I used to serve the people outside on the tables. I did everything.

I washed the dishes. I baked the pizzas. When I say everything, I mean everything. I enjoyed this job. Everyone was young and energetic with a nice smile on their face. I had a good time. After a few months of working there, I realized that I needed to make a change in my life. I decided to apply so I could get permission to travel outside of the United States, and I knew that if this permission were to get approved, I was not guaranteed to be able to come back into the United States, but I wanted to travel to my country so I could see my mom, my brother, my sister, and their kids. I was eager to take this trip. After finding out that my trip was approved, I almost immediately purchased the plane tickets. I flew to Guatemala in 2015, my first ever trip outside of the United

States, not knowing if I was even going to be able to make it back in here.

Have you ever made a decision that scared you? Have you ever had the desire to make something happen, but you knew in your gut that it could go wrong, and it was going to make every single plan you had disappear out of nowhere? I had that feeling, but the love for my family was bigger than the fear I had. After spending three weeks in Guatemala, I came back to the United States. I arrived at the airport in San Francisco, California to an immigration officer. He asked me a few questions that were not about my trip or myself. They were more friendly questions and I was able to connect with him almost immediately. When he stamped my approval to enter back into the country, I felt like this weight came off my shoulders. After living in the United States for a few days when I came back from Guatemala, I decided that it was time for me to get another job, so I went to work at Tesla through a third-party company. My position was that of a robot technician.

I worked there for about three months and a half because even though I was getting paid more money than I had ever been paid before at a job, I did not like supervisor's behavior. At the beginning of 2016, I decided to go back and study more, because education is the key to success. I found out about a program that would allow me to earn free college credits while being trained to be able to earn an internship at a multi-billion-dollar company, and I decided to apply for it. I would say that I am a very lucky person, because I was accepted into it. This program only allowed 18 to 24-year-olds in it, and I was already 24 years old. If I had waited a few more months, I would not have made it into the program, and I would not have gotten the experience that I got in a multi-billion-dollar company called Sales Force in San Francisco, California. After training at that program for about five months in project coordination, I earned my internship in Sales Force and my position there was as an onboarding coordinator.

I was there every day from 8:00 a.m. to 5:00 p.m. I met a lot of cool people. I must say I was amazed. I felt like I was on top of the world, but this, as easy as it may sound, was not that easy. During my first five months training for project coordination, I was working at night. I was driving a Bobtail truck, an 18-feet truck, white collar, and I was getting paid cash. I would get up at 1:00 a.m., take the truck at 2:00 a.m., get off work at 6:00 a.m., take a shower, and be in school by 8:00 a.m., then get off my training at 3:30 p.m., do my work, and then go to sleep, then go to work again at 1:00 in the morning. That was my schedule during my training. Then during my internship, it changed. I decided that I needed to rest so I made a commitment to stick to my internship from 8:00 a.m. to 5:00 p.m., then work at the pizzeria that I used to work at before on the weekends. Even though I was making very little money, I managed my way through the whole internship for six months.

In January 2017, I graduated, finally, with college credits, with a technical training program, and with a successfully completed internship at a multi-billion-dollar company. I was ready to continue my education, so I signed up at University of the People, where I am currently now working towards my bachelor's degree in business administration. This is my life story highlighted in details. There are so many things I could share with you that will make you realize how hard it actually is. Now that you're reading my book, it may seem like I have already made it, but I want to share with you, as the leader that I consider myself to be, that times are tough. Disappointments happen to all of us. The struggle is real. The challenges are big, but I am reminded of a quote by Jim Rohn that says, "Do not wish life was easier. Wish you were better." As a leader that you are, I am asking you, what are some skills that you can develop from now on that can help you make your life much easier? Work on that.

Those skills will dramatically improve your life.

Continue reading, and I am going to share with you some ways that you can improve your life and enhance your skills, learn new skills, and hopefully make your life even better than I hope it is today.

"I never lose. I either win or learn."

~ Nelson Mandela

What strategies do you use, to adapt to a new
environment? Share your thoughts about this chapter.

_____

_____

_____

_____

_____

_____

_____

_____

_____

_____

_____

_____

_____

_____

_____

_____

_____

_____

_____

_____

_____

_____

_____

_____

_____

_____

_____

_____

_____

What strategies do you use, to adapt to a new
environment? Share your thoughts about this chapter.

_____
_____
_____
_____
_____
_____
_____
_____
_____
_____
_____
_____
_____
_____
_____
_____
_____
_____
_____
_____
_____
_____
_____
_____
_____
_____
_____
_____
_____
_____
_____

What strategies do you use, to adapt to a new
environment? Share your thoughts about this chapter.

_____

_____

_____

_____

_____

_____

_____

_____

_____

_____

_____

_____

_____

_____

_____

_____

_____

_____

_____

_____

_____

_____

_____

_____

_____

_____

_____

_____

_____

_____

_____

_____

_____

What strategies do you use, to adapt to a new environment? Share your thoughts about this chapter.

_____

_____

_____

_____

_____

_____

_____

_____

_____

_____

_____

_____

_____

_____

_____

_____

_____

_____

_____

_____

_____

_____

_____

_____

_____

_____

_____

_____

_____

_____

_____

_____

_____

What strategies do you use, to adapt to a new
environment? Share your thoughts about this chapter.

_____

_____

_____

_____

_____

_____

_____

_____

_____

_____

_____

_____

_____

_____

_____

_____

_____

_____

_____

_____

_____

_____

_____

_____

_____

_____

_____

_____

_____

_____

_____

CONNECT

Yes, it's been said that you cannot influence someone unless you connect with them first. In order for you to get to influence me as your student, as your peer, as your mentee, as your coachee, you have to get to know me first. Let me tell you personally how my culture works. In my culture we care about family. Most of our families are religiously focused. To connect with me find out how everyone in my family is doing. Talk to me about memories I can remember. Talk to me about memories I want to build. Ask me about the people I care most in my family. Ask me about my childhood. You see my culture has a lot of similarities with other cultures, so this should work across the border.

Ask me about my friends. Ask me about adventures. Ask me about how I am feeling. Sometimes I may be feeling good and sometimes I may be feeling bad, just like every human being. I am just like you, except that I may be younger than you, I may be more stubborn, I may have more grit than other people you have come across, but you won't find out about this unless you know me first through the people who I care about the most, which is my family. By finding out who my friends are, you will find out about who I am, because it's been said that we are the average of the five closest people in our lives.

Talk to me about academics. Even though this is probably not a priority for me at this point in my life, at a subconscious level I know that it is important in order to make my family proud and to succeed in society. Talk to me about the feeling of happiness that my loved ones will feel when I achieve high academic levels in my life. I will know, even if I don't accept it right now, I will know that this is true because I see it everywhere around me, I see it in movies, I see it in my peers, and I see it every day.

Now let me share with you some strategies of how you can connect with me. Find out about what holidays I celebrate with my family, and if you can make the time to attend one of my holiday celebrations. If you cannot find the time to attend one of my holiday celebrations, simply be present. Be present at one of my school events, even if it's just one. Make sure I see you. Make sure you stand out from the crowd. Make sure that you give me that "You've got this" look, and I will make sure to make a memory for myself because it is very important for me to know that you care. As I mentioned earlier in his book some people don't know about what you do unless they know who you are. Some people don't care about who you are unless they know why you do what you do. Therefore, I will know that you care for me because you've put in the time and effort to attend one of the holidays that I celebrate or one of the events that I am a part of.

Give me five minutes of your time if you can, just you and me, one-on-one. Conversations are very important. Even if I don't admit it at this point in my life, because I may show behavior consistent with rebels, behavior of being someone who does not listen, signs of being someone who does not understand, but subconsciously I know that this is good for me when you give me advice that is valuable, that brings hope to my life.

Be vulnerable with me. Share with me information

about the holidays you celebrate, the events you care about, the things that you like. Talk to me about your friends. The power of vulnerability allows us to connect at a much deeper level. High level conversations are businesslike, and I want to build with you a personal relationship. Remind me of your why and I will know that you care.

As you read this book I want to encourage you. I want to encourage you to focus on the good, because we young people seek hope. We persevere. We are a sponge. We have grit. We may not display these characteristics all at once or every day, but we know that it is important for us to move forward, to look forward to the future, that it is important for us to make our family proud. We know the effort that our parents make in order for them to provide for us the education that we have, in order for us to be able to get the things that we get in our daily basis, even if they seem basic like food and clothing. We see the effort that our loved ones put in so we succeed personally, and we can see the future where we can discover professional achievement in our lives.

We persevere. We have learned very early in our lives by watching our loved ones working hard day after day after day how they persevere. We learn by modeling after those who we love most. We're not afraid to work. Even though we may show sometimes signs of laziness, we are truly not afraid to work. We are strong and we will persevere if we just find that one caring adult that will show us the way.

We are a sponge. We observe. We read. We listen to music that gives us a message for us to learn. Yes, sometimes this music has a message that we don't need in our lives, but we are still trying to learn what these message means to us. We are a sponge. Take advantage that our mind is fresh. Take advantage that our mind is not yet full of content where your message will get lost. Our mind is ready to learn from you if you just show us that you care.

We have grit. We combine perseverance, attitude, courage, and strength in order for us to have the grit that we have. We will be stubborn about what we want. Sometimes it may seem like what we want is not the best for us, but I want you to focus in the quality of this characteristic. We may be stubborn about something that is not good for us in our lives right now, but please help us figure out how to use these characteristics towards the positive things in our lives. Help us analyze. Help us use this grit, to take advantage of it and make the best out of it for our own good for our future.

Trust me you are a change-maker. You are a positive influence in our lives. You are the person that brings hope even if we sometimes do not express it, even if we sometimes do not show gratitude for it, and we know that you know deeply in your heart. Keep doing what you're doing. Encourage us, motivate us. Show us the value of your leadership and we will follow.

What strategies will you use to connect with new people?
Share your thoughts about this chapter.

_____

_____

_____

_____

_____

_____

_____

_____

_____

_____

_____

_____

_____

_____

_____

_____

_____

_____

_____

_____

_____

_____

_____

_____

_____

_____

_____

_____

_____

What strategies will you use to connect with new people?
Share your thoughts about this chapter.

_____

_____

_____

_____

_____

_____

_____

_____

_____

_____

_____

_____

_____

_____

_____

_____

_____

_____

_____

_____

_____

_____

_____

_____

_____

_____

_____

_____

_____

_____

What strategies will you use to connect with new people?
Share your thoughts about this chapter.

_____

_____

_____

_____

_____

_____

_____

_____

_____

_____

_____

_____

_____

_____

_____

_____

_____

_____

_____

_____

_____

_____

_____

_____

_____

_____

_____

_____

_____

_____

What strategies will you use to connect with new people?
Share your thoughts about this chapter.

_____

_____

_____

_____

_____

_____

_____

_____

_____

_____

_____

_____

_____

_____

_____

_____

_____

_____

_____

_____

_____

_____

_____

_____

_____

_____

_____

_____

_____

_____

_____

What strategies will you use to connect with new people?
Share your thoughts about this chapter.

_____
_____
_____
_____
_____
_____
_____
_____
_____
_____
_____
_____
_____
_____
_____
_____
_____
_____
_____
_____
_____
_____
_____
_____
_____
_____
_____
_____
_____
_____
_____
_____
_____

INSPIRE

Inspire me, tell me a story about courage so I know that there are possibilities, far more than what I imagined for my life at this point. Show me a motivational video, motivation is very important for all of us, even if It isn't apparent to me right now. This is the moment where I need motivation the most.

Introduce me to a successful person, success means different things to different people. Usually, after a conversation with me about my family, my culture, the things that matter to me, I am sure you will have a feel of what a successful person would look like to me. If you still can't figure it out, go ahead and ask me. You never know until you ask. Ask me what a successful person looks like to me. If you can, do introduce me to someone with that similar profile of what I will describe to you. Introduce me to a person in my career of interest. If I don't know what I want to do with my life yet, introduce me to several people in different career paths. Introduce me to these people so I get a chance to ask them personal questions about how they figured out what they wanted to do with their lives. These things are common sense, but may not be common practice for a lot of people.

Gift me a book, a book of inspiration, a book on courage, a book on motivation, a book that tells a real story of someone who made it against the odds. This book can be an audiobook, this book can be a physical book, or this book can be an e-book. Even if it's a used book from the thrift store, even if it's a book that was given to you earlier in your life and you want to now pass it on to me, it could potentially change my life for the better. This will give me a hint that you truly care about me. Even if I don't express it openly, I will know deep within my heart that you are that one caring adult that I need in my life.

Help me see a vision of what is possible for me. You are aware of the environment I grew up in based on what you have gleaned from me. You know what is possible in this environment. Encourage me if I need to grow in this area or if I need to look for a new place to explore, if I need to move on to where there is opportunity for me. For example, if I want to be in tech, I could be in Houston, Texas. If I want to be in tech, I could be in San Francisco, California, Silicon Valley. If I want to be in tech, I could live in Pittsburgh. If I want to be in tech, I could live in Ohio. These are all different options that I probably haven't even thought of unless you bring it up to me if I am interested in tech. If I am interested in different fields, please help me see what is possible for me locally and out of state.

You can encourage me by telling me a story about courage, and this story can be based on a person with a similar background to mine. Tell me a personal story of your own courage. This will help me get inspired by you to know that you've been there through the struggle, to know that you have made it against all odds, to know that you feel what it feels like to be in a similar situation to mine.

Show me a motivational video on YouTube. There are a lot of different videos available online now for free. All you have to do is go the extra-mile. Look for the one perfect video that will make my day. Look for that one video that will make me envision myself as a better person than I am today. Show me this motivational video that will light up the fire in me and will help me thrive, will help me go from feeling like a victim to feeling like a victor. Show me, and I will remember.

Introduce me to a potential mentor. Whenever you show me a person of success, ask them if they can mentor me. Ask them if they can meet with me once or twice a month for 30 minutes or one hour. This could dramatically change my life because this person could be the messenger I need. Besides you being the leader that I need, this person could be the messenger that I need in my life to help guide me through what I am going into. Show me a coach. Show me that one person that has been in my shoes and has made it to the career path of their choice. This person can give me the practical guidance that I need. This person can tell me what exactly I need to do and not do so I can develop myself to a level where I can achieve my personal and professional goals. Show me a coach that can teach me discipline. Show me a coach that will let me know what is possible through personal effort.

Show me the numbers. Show me what it will be like when I make it to my desired goal. How much money will I make? How much money is possible for me to make locally? How much income can I make outside of my current state? Tell me. Break it down for me weekly, monthly. Tell me how it can make a humongous difference in my life.

Yes, you may think to yourself, "Wow. Well, this is a little bit too much." But this is really what I need. I don't really think about this daily sometimes. I may not express that I need this in my life. You may even think that this should be common sense, but for me, having different situations in my life, trying to juggle family, school, and work sometimes can become very frustrating and oftentimes super overwhelming. I may be tired of feeling this way, but I don't express it. I need that caring adult, you, the leader, that will connect with me, that will inspire me to see that which I am not showing outside, that which I am not showing to the outside world.

I am counting on you. You are the one who can truly make a difference in my life. You are the one that I will remember. Your legacy will live for generations and generations. This is you moment to make a truly positive impact in my life. I am open. I am willing to learn. I am a sponge. I am the student that is ready, and I know you are the teacher that has now appeared. Let's do this together. I understand that teamwork makes the dream work. I understand that winners never quit and quitters never win. I understand that I am born to win. I may not know it consciously yet, I may not assume it yet, but subconsciously I know I was born to win.

How do you plan to inspire others?
Share your thoughts about this chapter.

_____

_____

_____

_____

_____

_____

_____

_____

_____

_____

_____

_____

_____

_____

_____

_____

_____

_____

_____

_____

_____

_____

_____

_____

_____

_____

_____

_____

_____

_____

_____

_____

How do you plan to inspire others?
Share your thoughts about this chapter.

_____

_____

_____

_____

_____

_____

_____

_____

_____

_____

_____

_____

_____

_____

_____

_____

_____

_____

_____

_____

_____

_____

_____

_____

_____

_____

_____

_____

_____

_____

_____

_____

_____

How do you plan to inspire others?
Share your thoughts about this chapter.

_____

_____

_____

_____

_____

_____

_____

_____

_____

_____

_____

_____

_____

_____

_____

_____

_____

_____

_____

_____

_____

_____

_____

_____

_____

_____

_____

_____

_____

_____

_____

_____

_____

How do you plan to inspire others?
Share your thoughts about this chapter.

_____
_____
_____
_____
_____
_____
_____
_____
_____
_____
_____
_____
_____
_____
_____
_____
_____
_____
_____
_____
_____
_____
_____
_____
_____
_____
_____
_____
_____
_____
_____

How do you plan to inspire others?
Share your thoughts about this chapter.

_____

_____

_____

_____

_____

_____

_____

_____

_____

_____

_____

_____

_____

_____

_____

_____

_____

_____

_____

_____

_____

_____

_____

_____

_____

_____

_____

_____

_____

_____

_____

_____

LEAD

Show me by example. This is how I will best learn from you. The books, the videos, they are all great, but I want to see you working your magic. Maybe you do not have every skill, every characteristic that I am looking for, but show me how you use what you have to become the person you have become. I want to understand how you understand people and human nature. Give me an example so I can begin to think for myself. Show me how you talk to people. One way that you can show me is by talking to me and that's how I will learn. Show me how you make people feel important. Again, one way I can learn is by observing how you make me feel important right now. Show me how you agree with people with whom you sometimes do not necessarily agree with 100%. Show me how to skillfully listen to people. One way I will learn this is by observing how you listen to me. But I want to know how you listen to other people as well.

How do you influence people? Maybe the way you influence me is not the same way you influence other people. I want to learn how to deal with different people. Show me how you do it. How do you convince people? How do you help people make up their mind? How do you help people set their moods so that they can achieve their own personal goals? Maybe through changing their mentality, to changing their psychology, so they can then change their thinking. How do you do it? I want to see you do it. Give me a chance to see you. How do you praise people for their achievements? I want to learn, I want to see it in action.

I am looking for you to lead me by example. I depend on you at this point in my life. I trust you. Even if I may not express it daily, even if I may not express it as often as I should, I trust you, that's why I listen to you, and I am watching, how do you make a good impression? How do you skillfully make first impressions? How do you carry yourself? I know that you have skills that you may not be sharing with me consciously, but I am learning from you at a subconscious level.

I want to know how to start a conversation. I want to know how to motivate other people. Share with me some tips. Express how you display your genuine interest in others. I am observing. I am a sponge. I am motivated. I will use these skills that you are sharing with me to the best of my ability so I can achieve my own personal and professional success. I will focus on my education by teaming up with you on a daily basis, as often as possible, to work on these skills, because if I want to become more I have to learn more, and I am ready to learn.

Show me, how do you handle mistakes? How do you deal with complaints? How do you accept constructive criticisms? These skills I want to learn from you. You are the person that is truly making a difference in my life. I am interested in knowing how you set your own personal goals. How did you achieve your own professional goals? I want to be instructed on how to focus and how to be disciplined. Show me how you do it personally. I want to connect with you.

I am a young person who's ready to learn. I want to know how you achieve your balance between work and personal life, so I can apply these principles between my work, my school, and my personal life. Should I separate them all? Or should I integrate them all together? I want to know, how do you keep a positive mental attitude even though sometimes things don't go your way? You are the leader I am looking up to. I want to know how you deal with worry and stress. I want to know what mental capacity I need to have in order for me not to be overtaken by worry.

I want to get inspired by your enthusiasm, by that sparkle of life that you bring in. I want to learn how to be a light whenever I come into a dark room. I want to be your student. I am ready to learn. I will be patient, because I know everything has a purpose. You know in yourself that I am intelligent beyond what other people think of me at this point in my life. You know me well. You know that I am resilient and that I will act with no regret. You know I am ready to learn if you just take the time to inspire me, to coach me, and to lead me.

I want to learn from you how you manage stress. I want to learn how you build your own personal self-confidence. I want to learn how you have empathy for people, how to have class and confidence in every situation possible. And even if you don't know every skill that I am asking for you to show me, introduce me to someone who can show me these skills, so that I can be ready for the real world. Show me how you take fear and turn it into courage. I want you to lead me by example. Show me how to achieve productivity beyond what I can possibly think is possible for me right now.

Talk to me about money, things that are essential in my life. Introduce me to an accountant so that I know how to deal with different situations that I will go through my entire life. These skills I ask from you, I do not expect to come only from you. I only have the hopes that you will introduce me to the right person at the right time, so that I can be ready and prepare. Please lead me by example. I promise I will make you proud. I promise your legacy will live on. I promise that I may be a young adult right now but my potential is unlimited. I challenge you to take the leap of faith in me, to go the extra mile, and I will flourish through your leadership.

How will you lead from now on?
Share your thoughts about this chapter.

_____

_____

_____

_____

_____

_____

_____

_____

_____

_____

_____

_____

_____

_____

_____

_____

_____

_____

_____

_____

_____

_____

_____

_____

_____

_____

_____

_____

_____

_____

_____

_____

How will you lead from now on?
Share your thoughts about this chapter.

_____

_____

_____

_____

_____

_____

_____

_____

_____

_____

_____

_____

_____

_____

_____

_____

_____

_____

_____

_____

_____

_____

_____

_____

_____

_____

_____

_____

_____

_____

How will you lead from now on?
Share your thoughts about this chapter.

_____

_____

_____

_____

_____

_____

_____

_____

_____

_____

_____

_____

_____

_____

_____

_____

_____

_____

_____

_____

_____

_____

_____

_____

_____

_____

_____

_____

How will you lead from now on?
Share your thoughts about this chapter.

_____
_____
_____
_____
_____
_____
_____
_____
_____
_____
_____
_____
_____
_____
_____
_____
_____
_____
_____
_____
_____
_____
_____
_____
_____
_____
_____
_____
_____
_____

How will you lead from now on?
Share your thoughts about this chapter.

_____

_____

_____

_____

_____

_____

_____

_____

_____

_____

_____

_____

_____

_____

_____

_____

_____

_____

_____

_____

_____

_____

_____

_____

_____

_____

_____

_____

_____

_____

_____

_____

MOTIVATION

Motivation is like bathing. It does not last forever. That is the main reason why Zig Ziglar recommended it every day.

Every time I deliver a motivational workshop to parents on how to raise positive kids in a negative world, parents ask me this question: "Do you go to schools to inspire and motivate kids?" The answer is "Yes". Parents recommend that I should go to every school possible. My response is: "Yes, I do motivate students, like myself. But it is the school that makes the final decision on whether or not I can come and motivate their students."

If you feel it would be a great idea for me to come and motivate your kids in their school, go ahead and recommend my workshop to the decision maker of that school or private organization. Many times, it is the Community Liaison, Parent Coordinator, the Principal, or event coordinator who makes the decision.

My story of overcoming adversity impacts them positively. Coming from the sugarcane fields of Guatemala to becoming a published author was not an easy task, especially because of my upbringing. I also speak in corporations, colleges, private organizations, churches, and every place where there are parents and/or entrepreneurs. Feel free to acquire a book as a gift for your loved one.

What do I talk about when I motivate students? I share with them my personal story. Once I have connected with them, I tell them what they want to hear and blend with it what they need to hear.

Overcoming adversity is a huge element in my talks because when students are in school, there are so many adversities for them to overcome that if they are not inspired and/or motivated to go through the finish line, they will quit. You do not want your kid to be a drop-out. Neither do I. I want you to be able to be at peace knowing your students are getting the necessary motivation and information for his or her transformation. Thank you! ¡Muchas Gracias!

Overall, what did you learn from this book?
Share your thoughts about this book.

_____

_____

_____

_____

_____

_____

_____

_____

_____

_____

_____

_____

_____

_____

_____

_____

_____

_____

_____

_____

_____

_____

_____

_____

_____

_____

_____

_____

_____

_____

_____

Overall, what did you learn from this book?
Share your thoughts about this book.

_____

_____

_____

_____

_____

_____

_____

_____

_____

_____

_____

_____

_____

_____

_____

_____

_____

_____

_____

_____

_____

_____

_____

_____

_____

_____

_____

_____

_____

_____

Overall, what did you learn from this book?
Share your thoughts about this book.

_____

_____

_____

_____

_____

_____

_____

_____

_____

_____

_____

_____

_____

_____

_____

_____

_____

_____

_____

_____

_____

_____

_____

_____

_____

_____

_____

_____

_____

Overall, what did you learn from this book?
Share your thoughts about this book.

_____

_____

_____

_____

_____

_____

_____

_____

_____

_____

_____

_____

_____

_____

_____

_____

_____

_____

_____

_____

_____

_____

_____

_____

_____

_____

_____

_____

_____

_____

_____

_____

Overall, what did you learn from this book?
Share your thoughts about this book.

_____

_____

_____

_____

_____

_____

_____

_____

_____

_____

_____

_____

_____

_____

_____

_____

_____

_____

_____

_____

_____

_____

_____

_____

_____

_____

_____

_____

_____

ABOUT THE AUTHOR

<u>Ovidilio David Vasquez</u> is the truest definition of a bootstrapper. From wielding a machete in the sugarcane fields of Guatemala at the tender age of 14, he emerges today as one of the most sought-after bilingual motivational speakers of our time. His story is unique and is the epitome of the American dream. He arrived in the US in 2006. In 2009, his mother had to return home to care for his dying grandmother. Left alone, with no support, Ovidilio did the only thing he could do—survive. Enrolled in high school during the day and working in warehouses at night, he overcame adversity and graduated in 2011. From there, he studied business management at Chabot College.

His crowning glory is that through his heart for migrant students, he was driven to high content motivational speaking and creating Speak Performance International, LLC. His signature talks are The Leader in You and The Brilliance in Resilience (for students) and How to Motivate Immigrant Students & Keep them Motivated (for educators) From there it was only upward and onward—in September 2014, this awesome speaker and humanitarian became a debut author. His books, THE PARENTING BOOK, WHO COACHES THE COACH, PONTE EN MIS ZAPATOS, and QUIEN ENTRENA AL ENTRENADOR are poised to be non-fiction runaway bestsellers. He shares with students overcome adversity through an entrepreneur mindset and emphasizes the importance of education.

If you were to ask Ovidilio the secret of his phenomenal success, he'd tell you he had a dream. He had no money, no social security number, no support—but he had a dream…and in accomplishing his dream he's able to motivate and inspire thousands around the world to achieve their dreams. Ovidilio D. Vasquez turned a life of lack into a world of abundance because he is unstoppable. In his own words, he shares his unwavering philosophy of life--"Education is THE KEY to success."

OVIDILIO DAVID VASQUEZ
A Farm Boy from the Sugarcane Fields of Central America

THE LEADER IN YOU

Inspiration for Migrant Students
and Those Who Educate Them

Made in the USA
Middletown, DE
14 March 2019